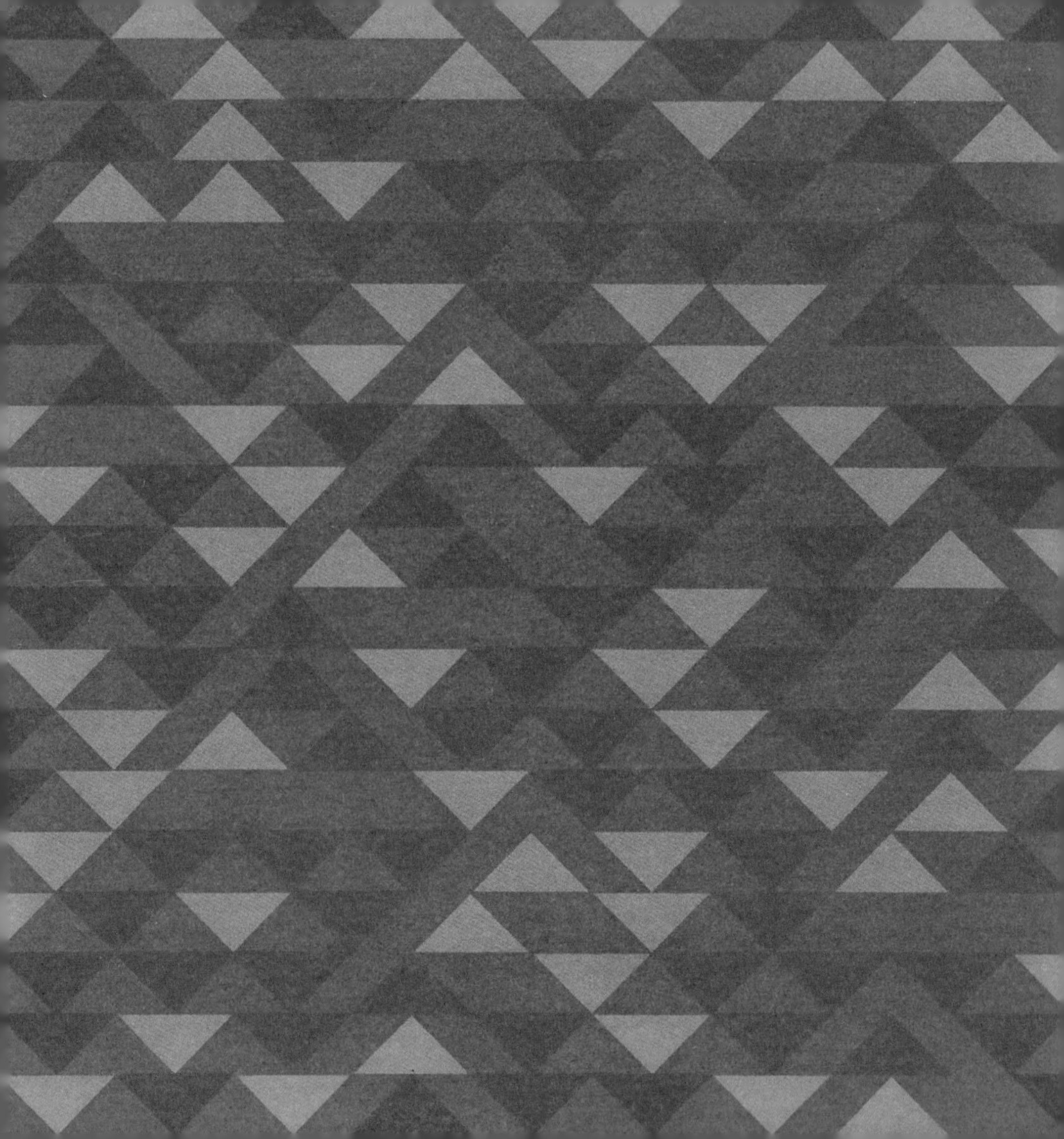

Artists Speak
Iconic Quotes on Modern Art

The Museum of Modern Art, New York

Making art has first of all to do with honesty.

Ellsworth Kelly

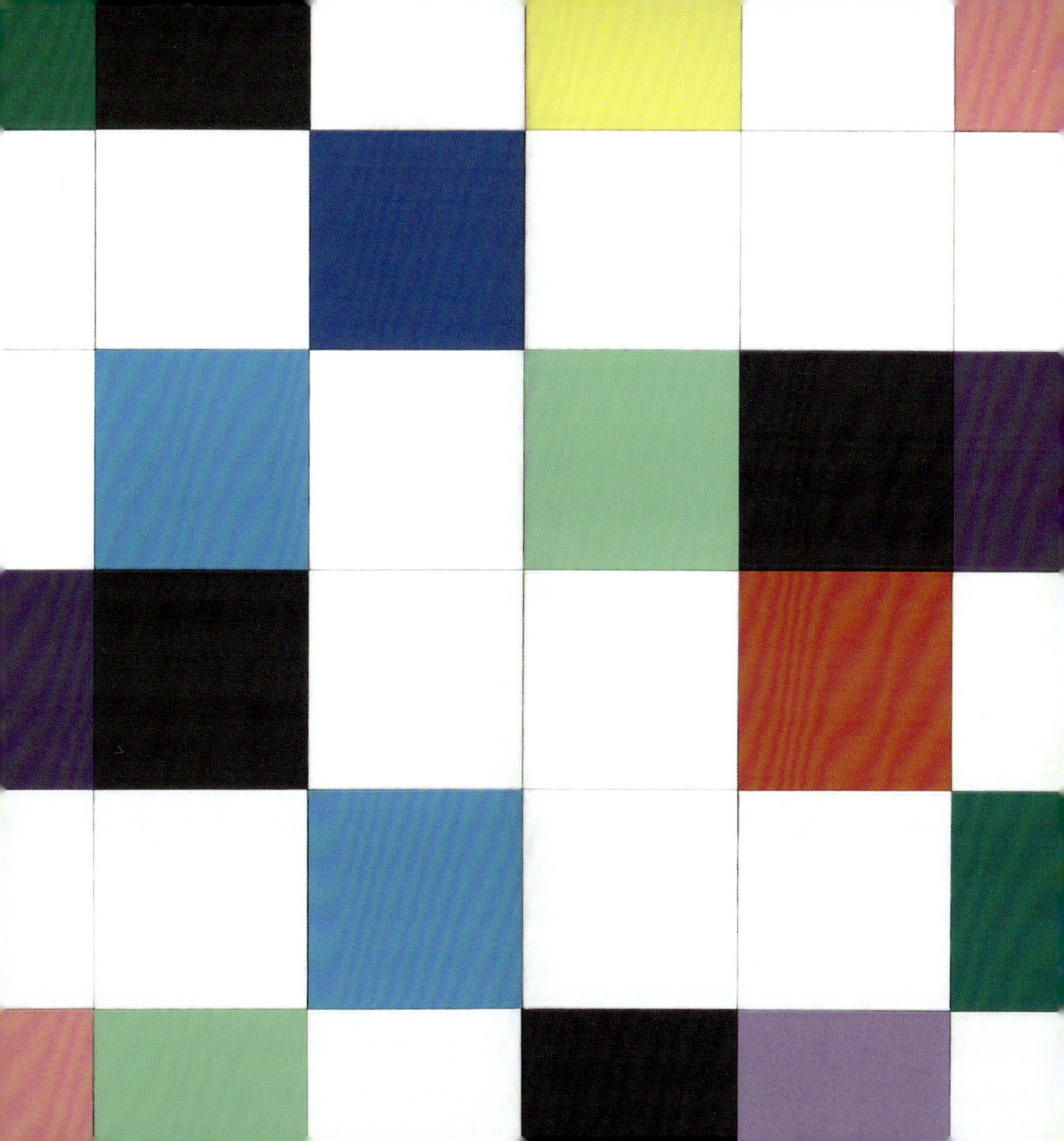

*Art is
something
that makes you
breathe with a
different kind
of happiness.*

Anni Albers

Art is total freedom.

Jack Whitten

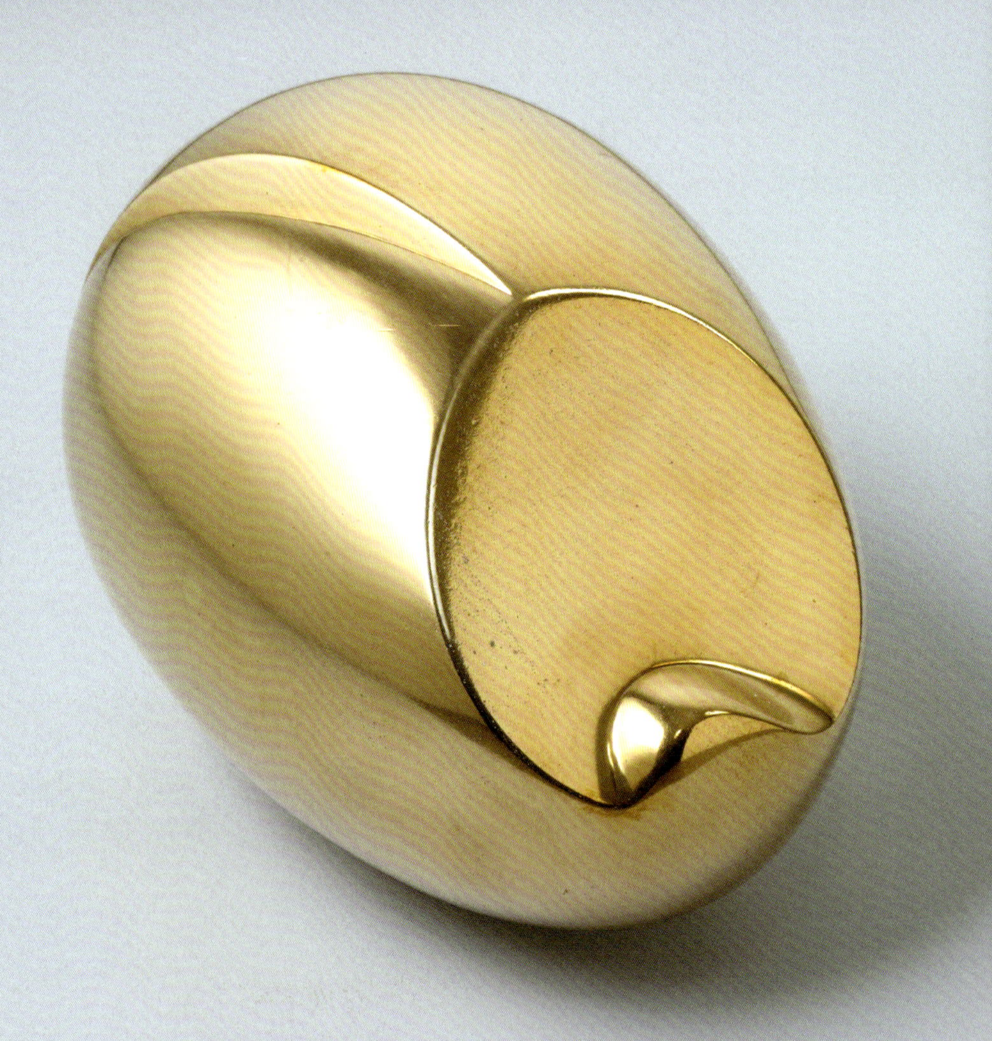

Art gives birth to ideas, it does not represent them.

Constantin Brancusi

*A true picture
has the power
to set the
imagination
to work.*

Wifredo Lam

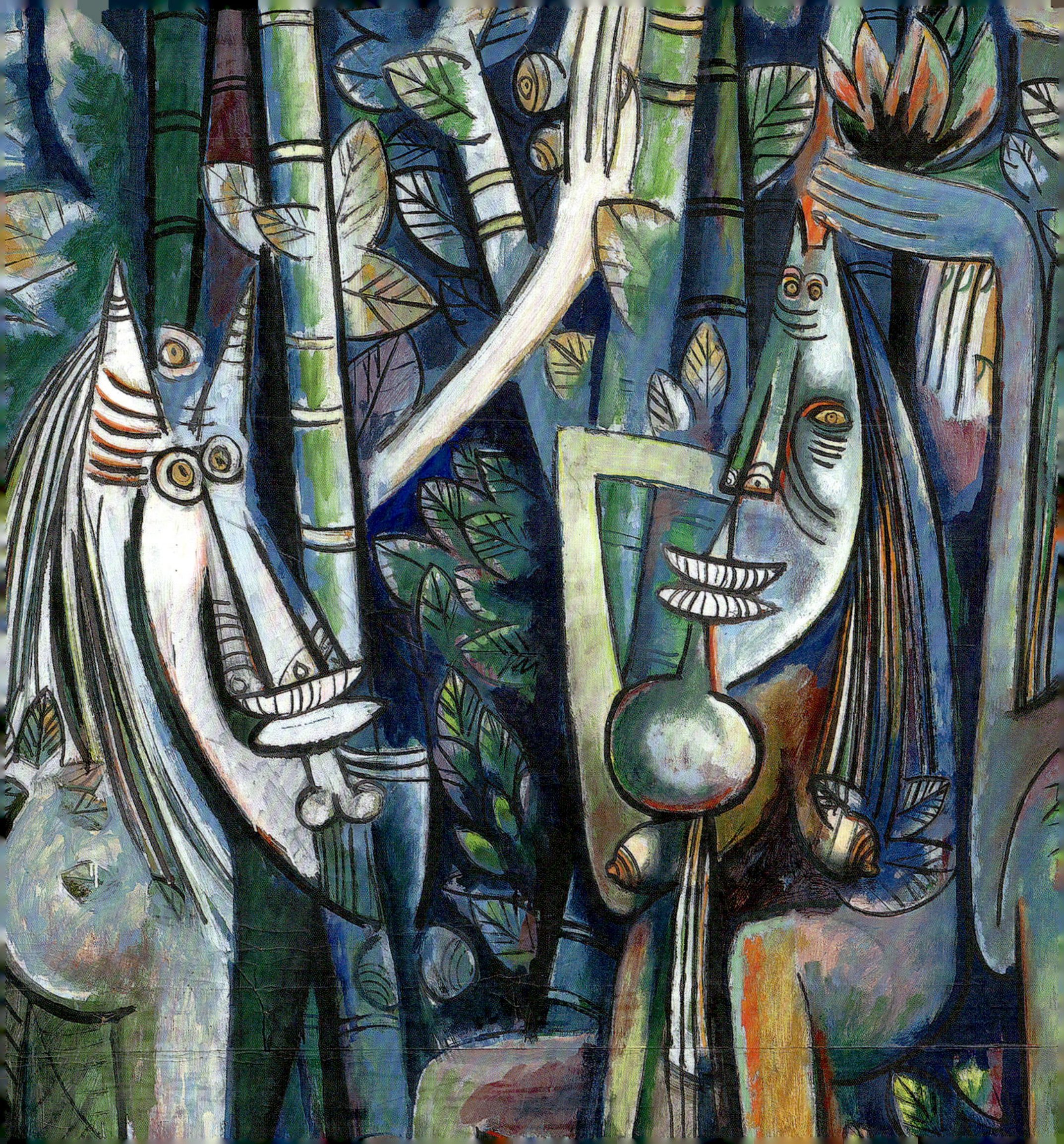

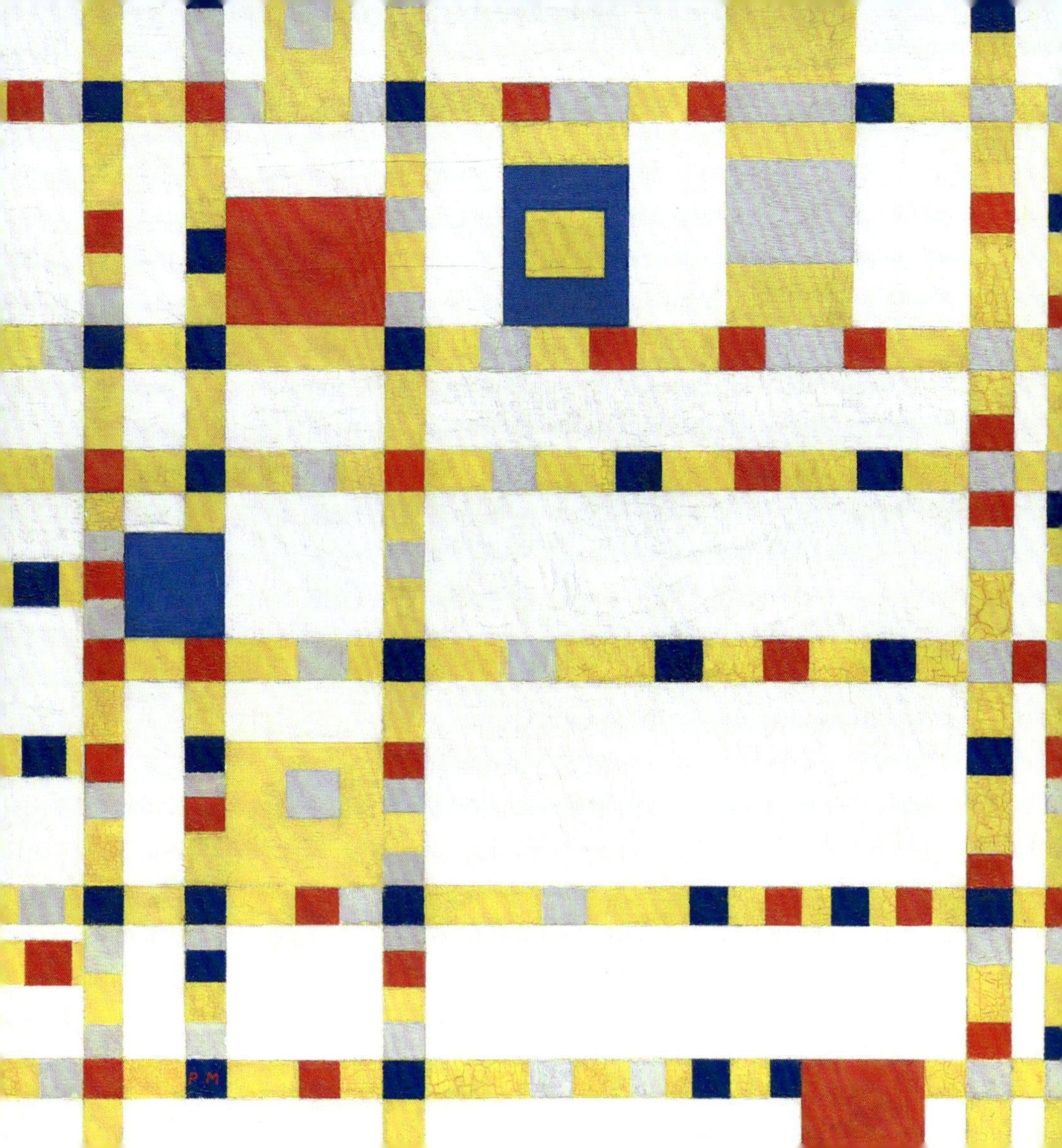
PM

I don't want pictures. I just want to find things out.

Piet Mondrian

I believe with my heart and soul in the power of the image.

Malick Sidibé

I believe in the balance between balance between dreaming and building.

Neri Oxman

*I found that
I could say things
with color and
shapes that
I couldn't say in
any other way.*

Georgia O'Keeffe

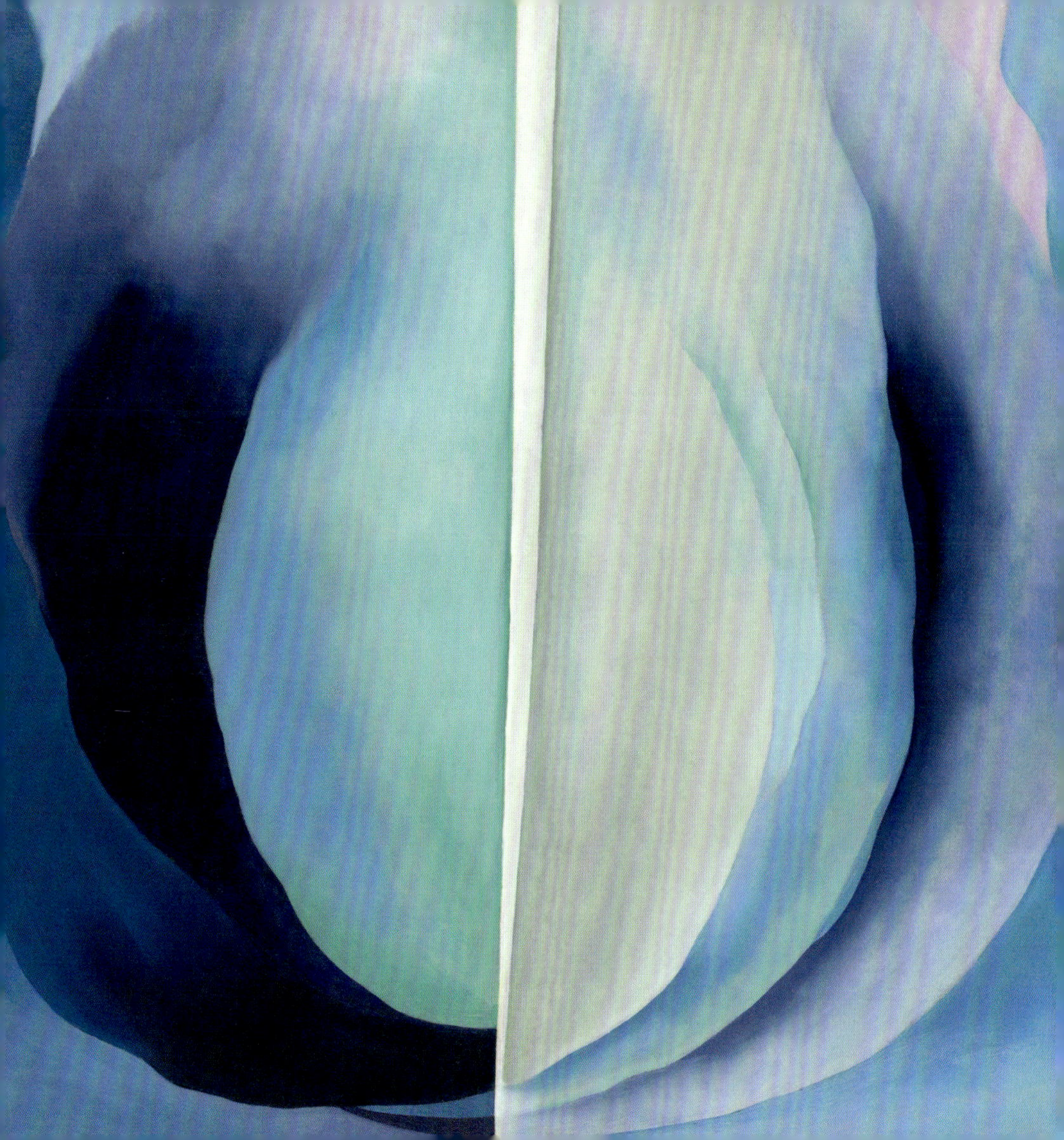

The wind has given me new colors through the windowpanes.

Alma Woodsey Thomas

Blue means you have left the drabness of day-to-day reality to be transported into . . . a world of freedom.

Louise Bourgeois

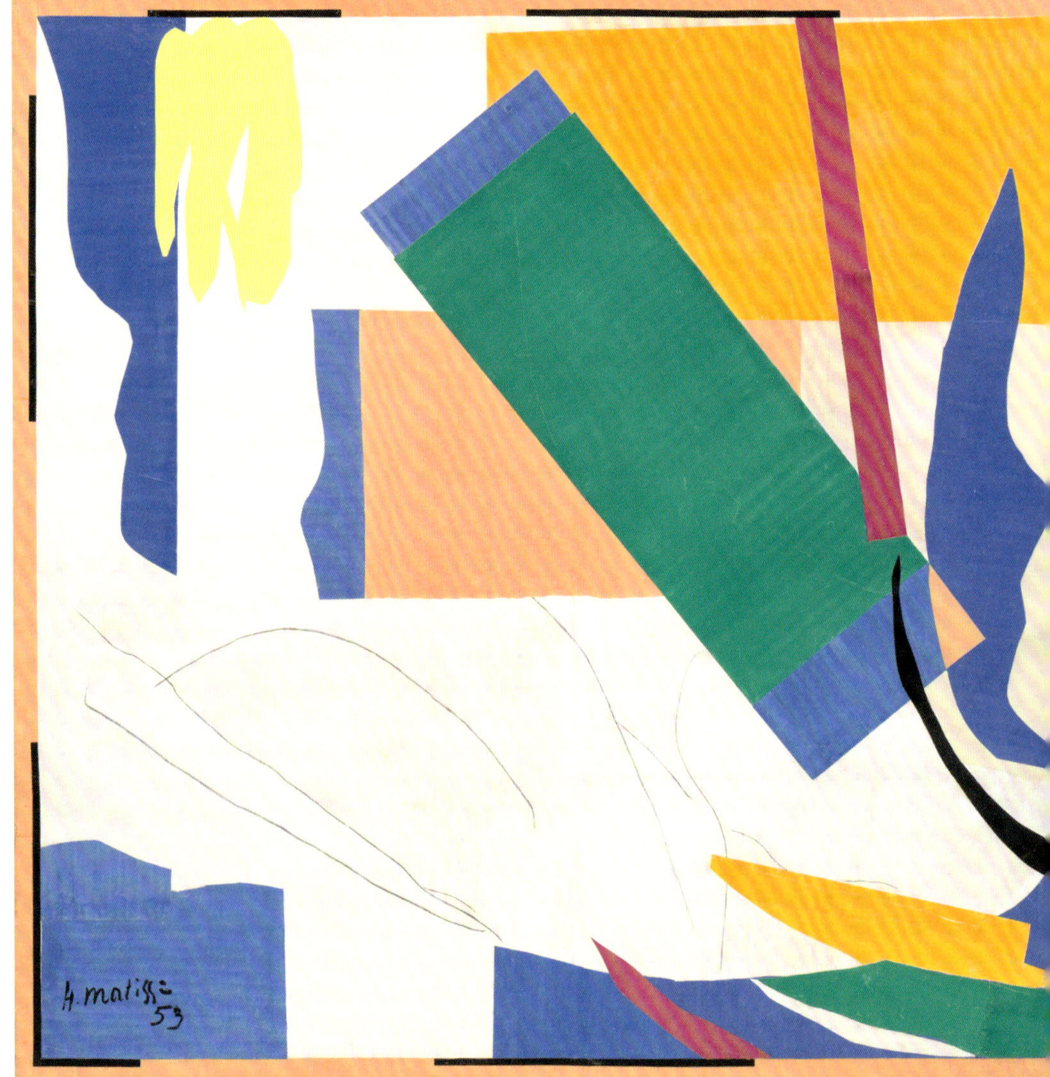

H. matisse
53

A certain blue enters your soul.

Henri Matisse

*I just happened
to paint words
like someone else
paints flowers.*

Ed Ruscha

I never know the photographs I will end up making.

An-My Lê

There is design in everything: in a cloud, in a fingerprint, in the sand, or in the sea.

Clara Porset

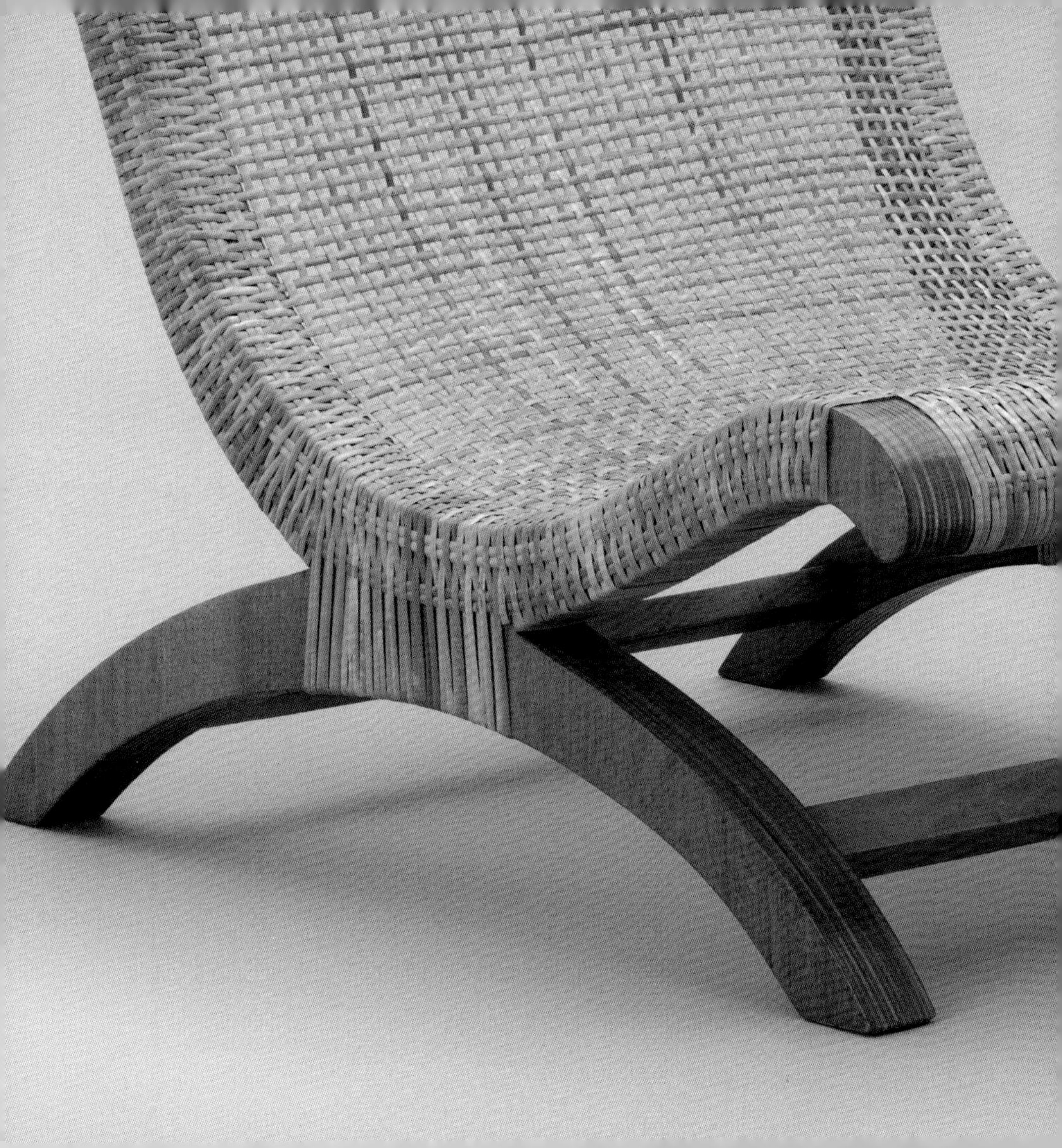

When you take something apart, you get a great sense of what it took to originally put it together.

Christian Marclay

Good design needs bad design and vice versa.

Ettore Sottsass

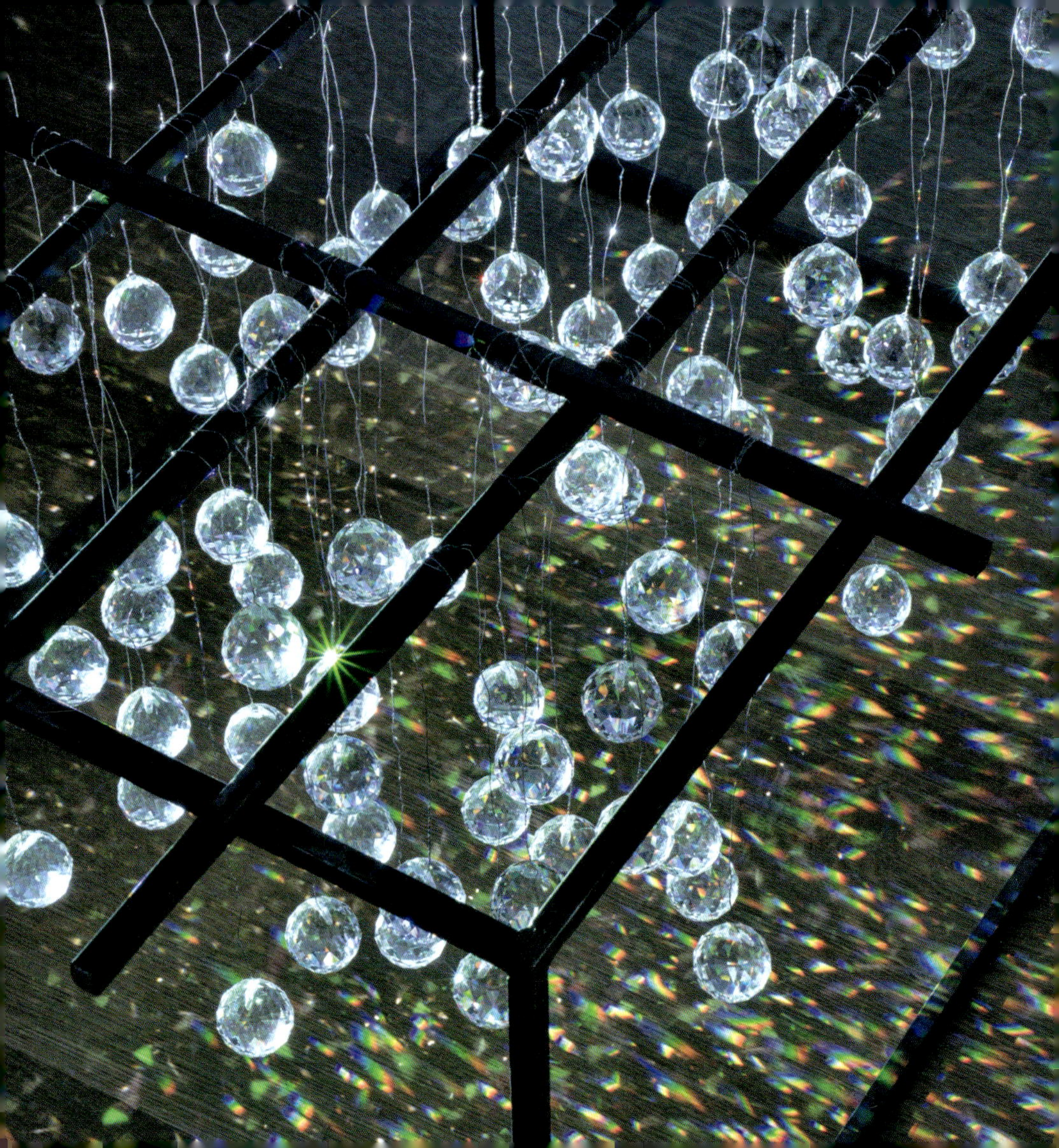

When you take something apart, you get a great sense of what it took to originally put it together.

Christian Marclay

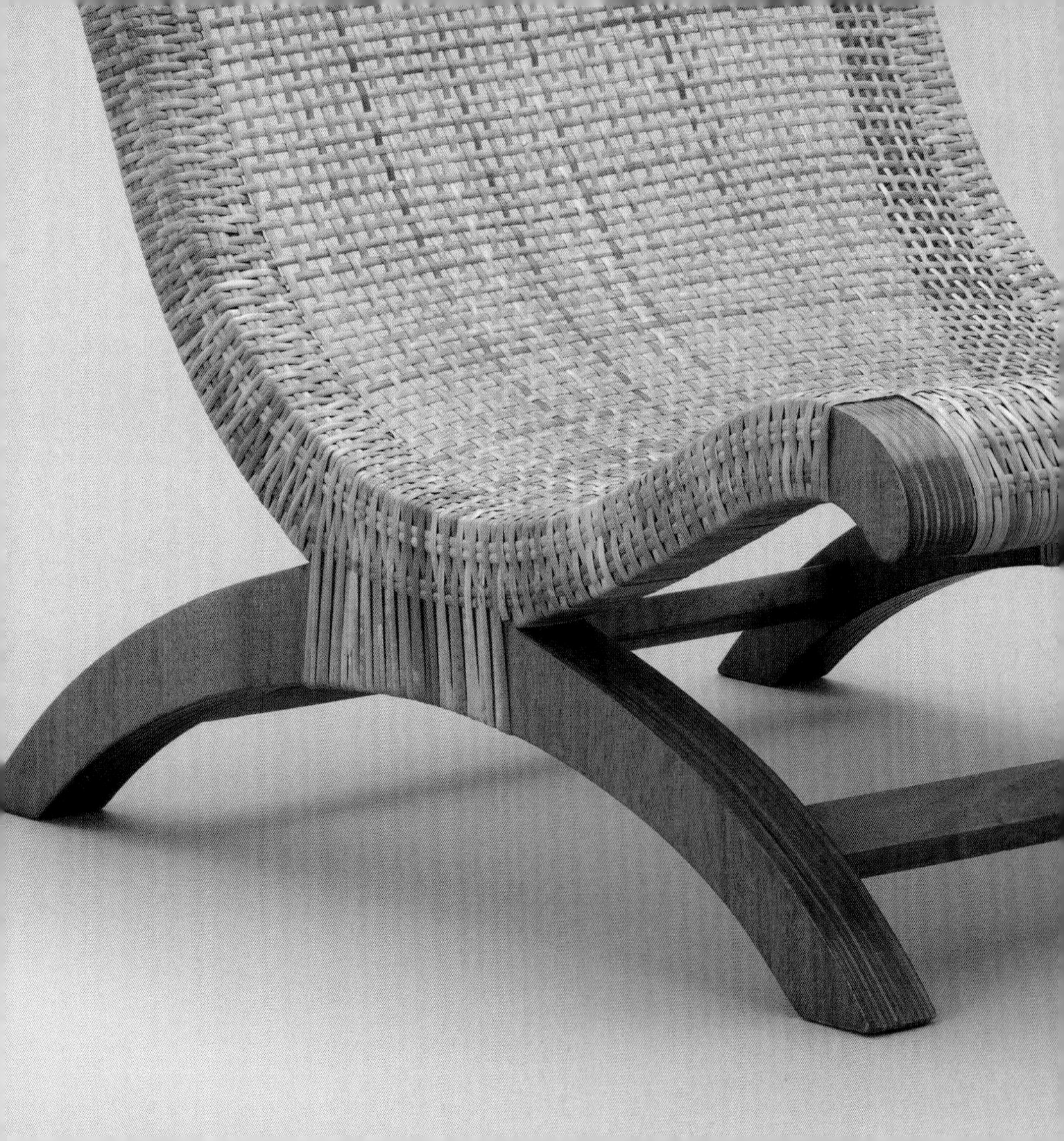

Every move depends on another.

Joan Jonas

I like to play with the possibilities of the limits I've made for myself.

Helen Frankenthaler

I don't want to
keep any rules.

Eva Hesse

There is a connection between the plant world and the world of the soul.

Hilma af Klint

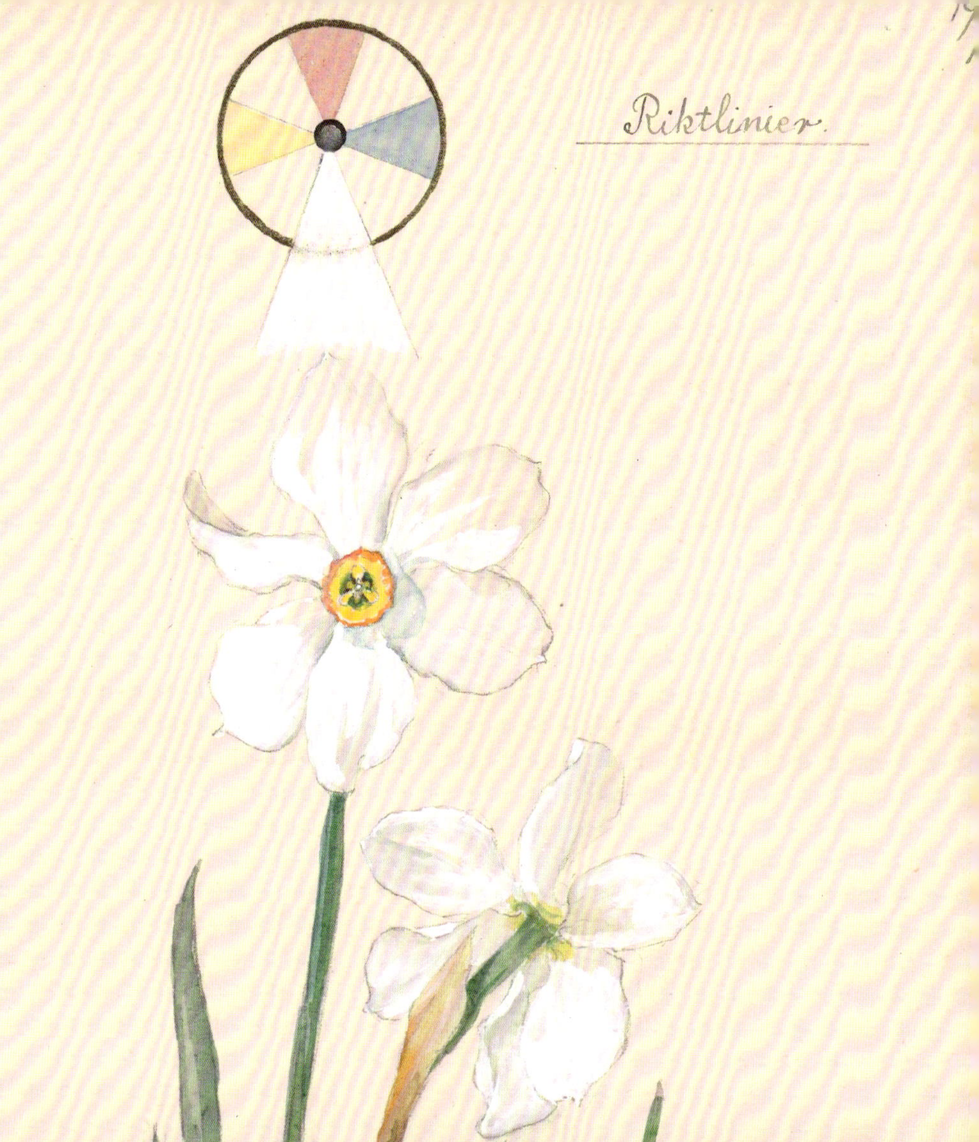

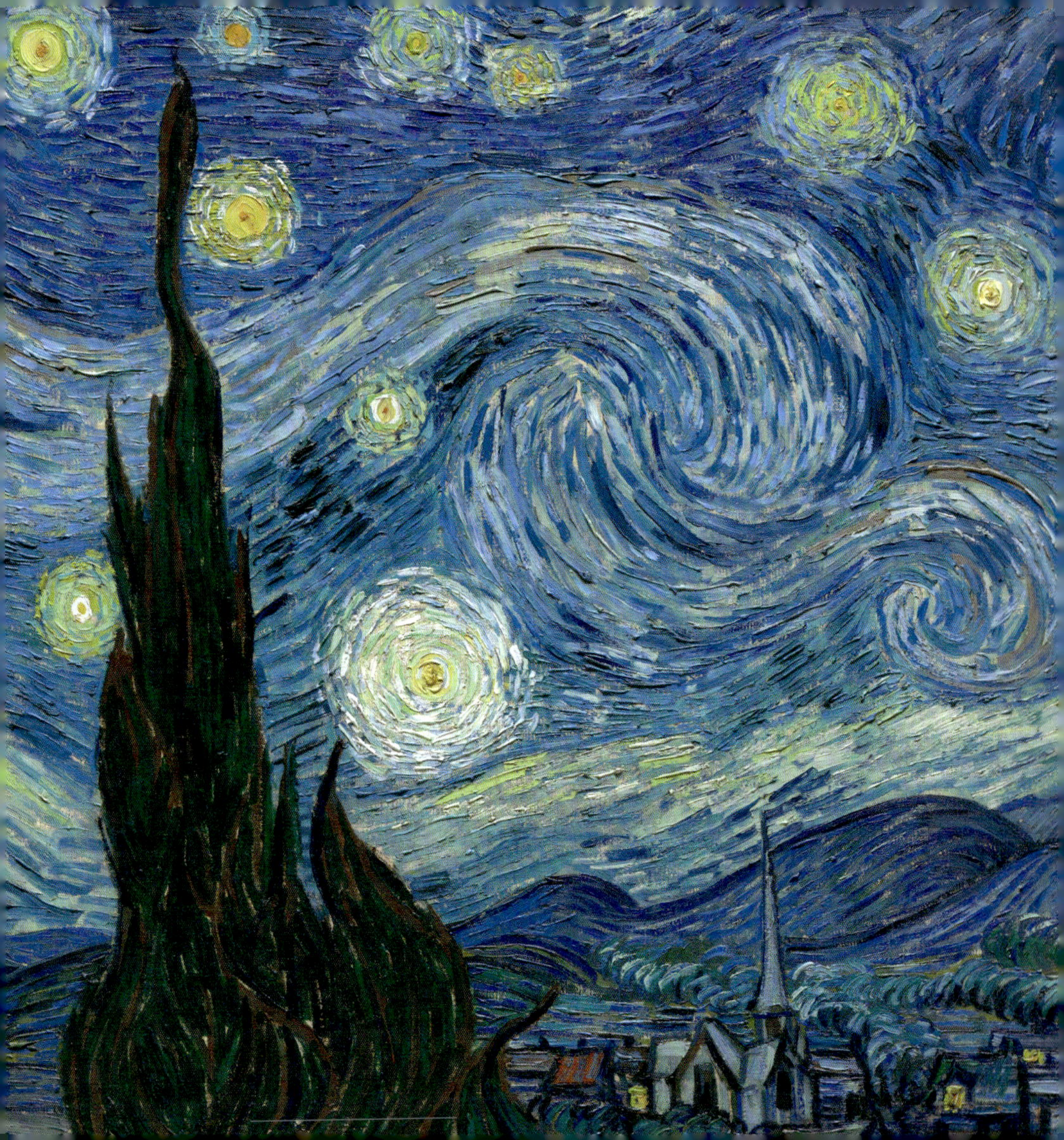

If one truly loves nature one finds beauty everywhere.

Vincent van Gogh

Open the
window and
count the stars.

Nam June Paik

Take your pleasure seriously.

Charles and Ray Eames

Art is much less important than life, but what a poor life without it!

Robert Motherwell

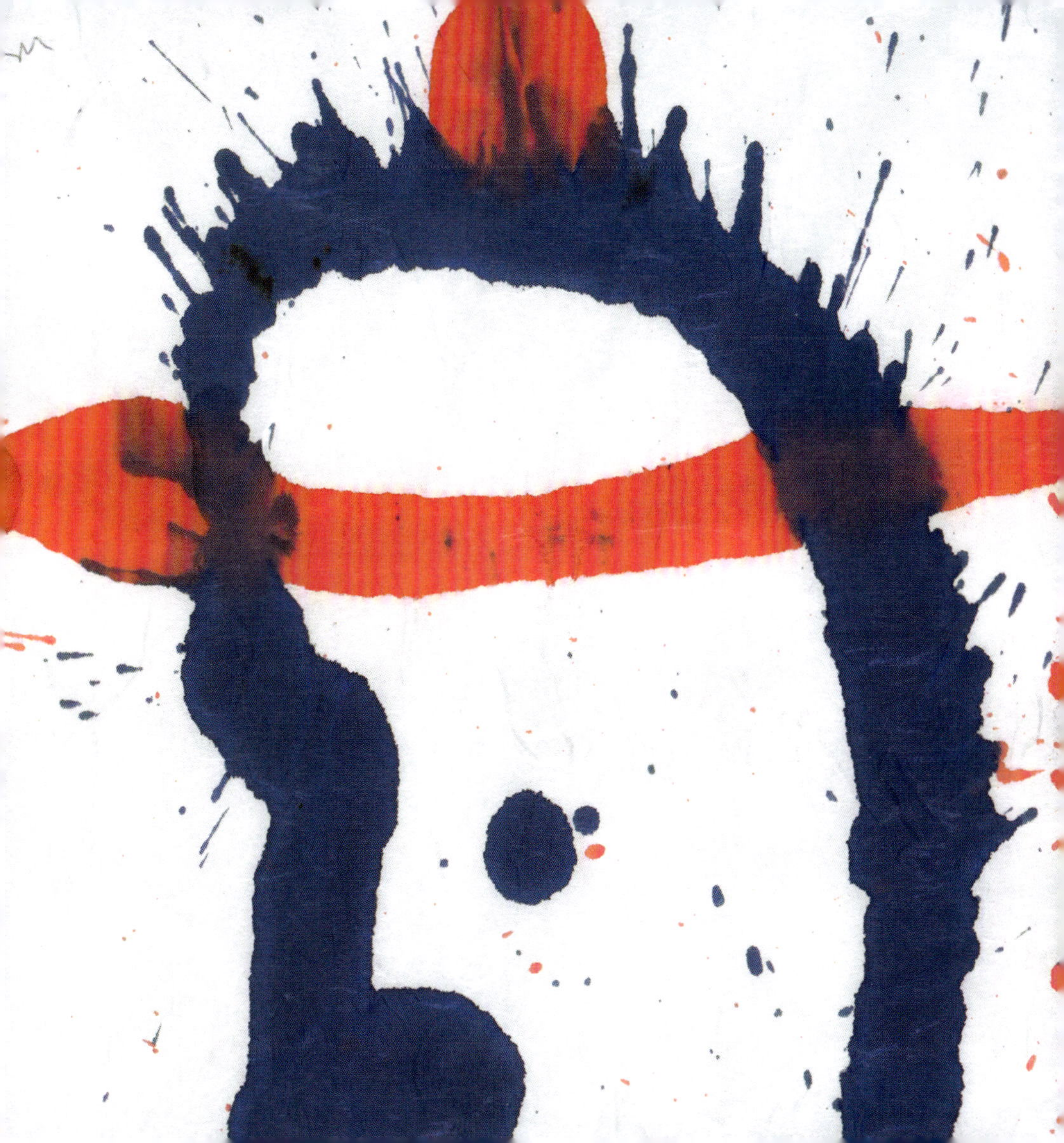

I can't understand
why people
are frightened
of new ideas.
I'm frightened of
the old ones.

John Cage

We are breaking with the past, because we cannot accept its hypotheses.

Liubov Popova

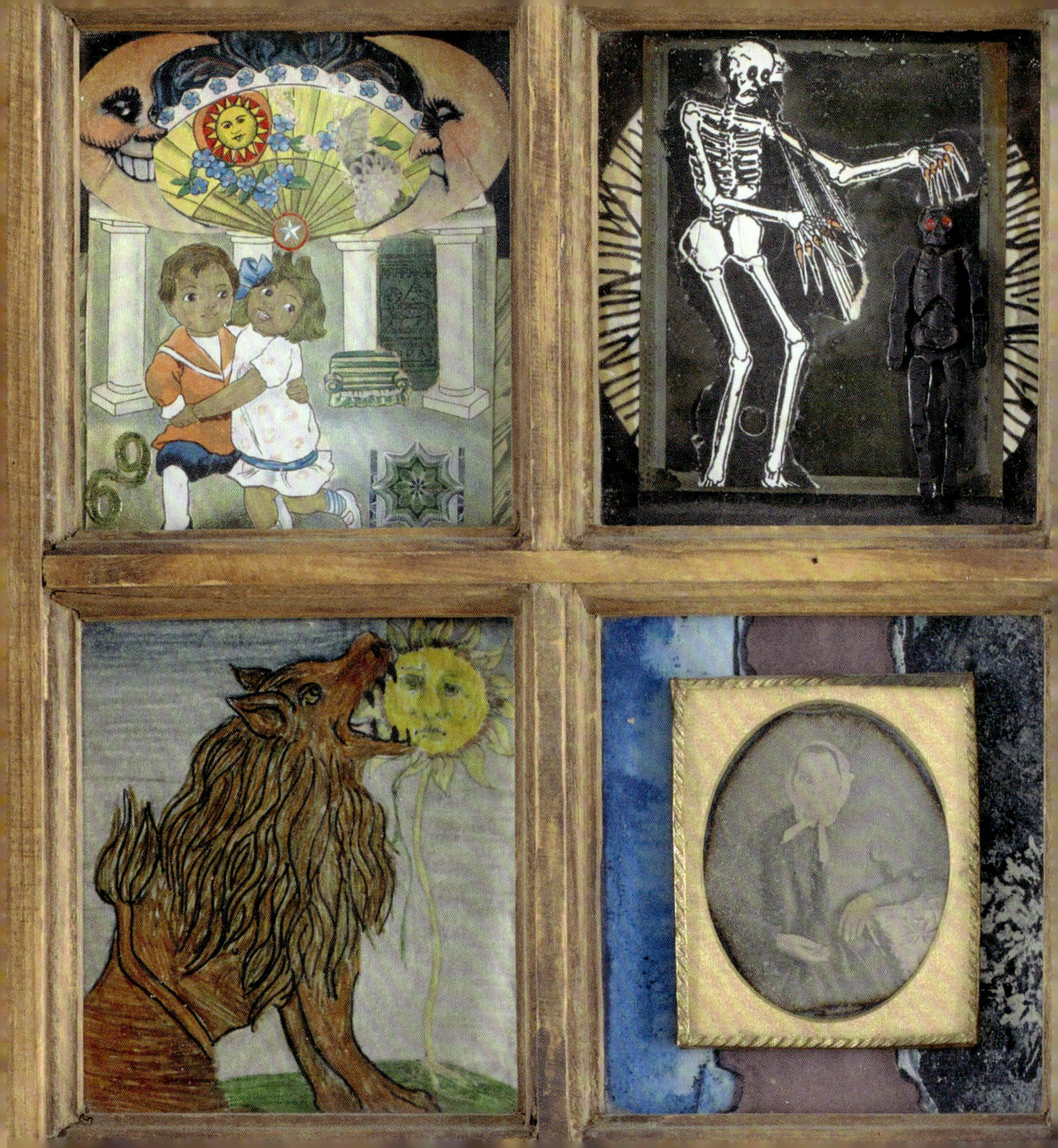

I learned early on that you can make art out of anything.

Betye Saar

The creative act is not performed by the artist alone.

Marcel Duchamp

We show who we are more clearly through our fiction than most anything else in our lives.

Guillermo del Toro

We are changed after we experience art. We see the world differently.

Milton Glaser

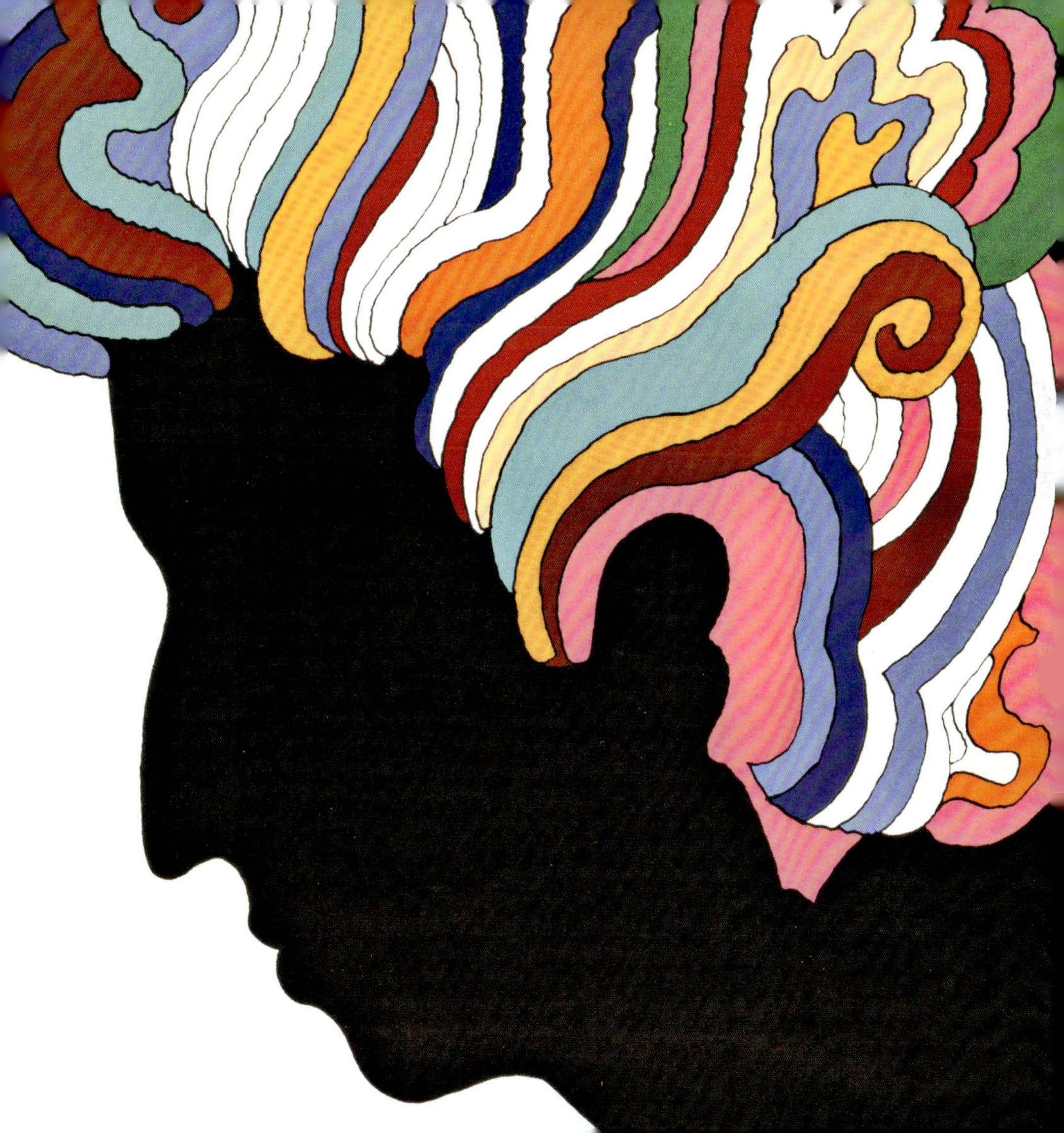

Social action gives the imagination a reason to get up in the morning.

Pope.L

Art is intrinsically political.

LaToya Ruby Frazier

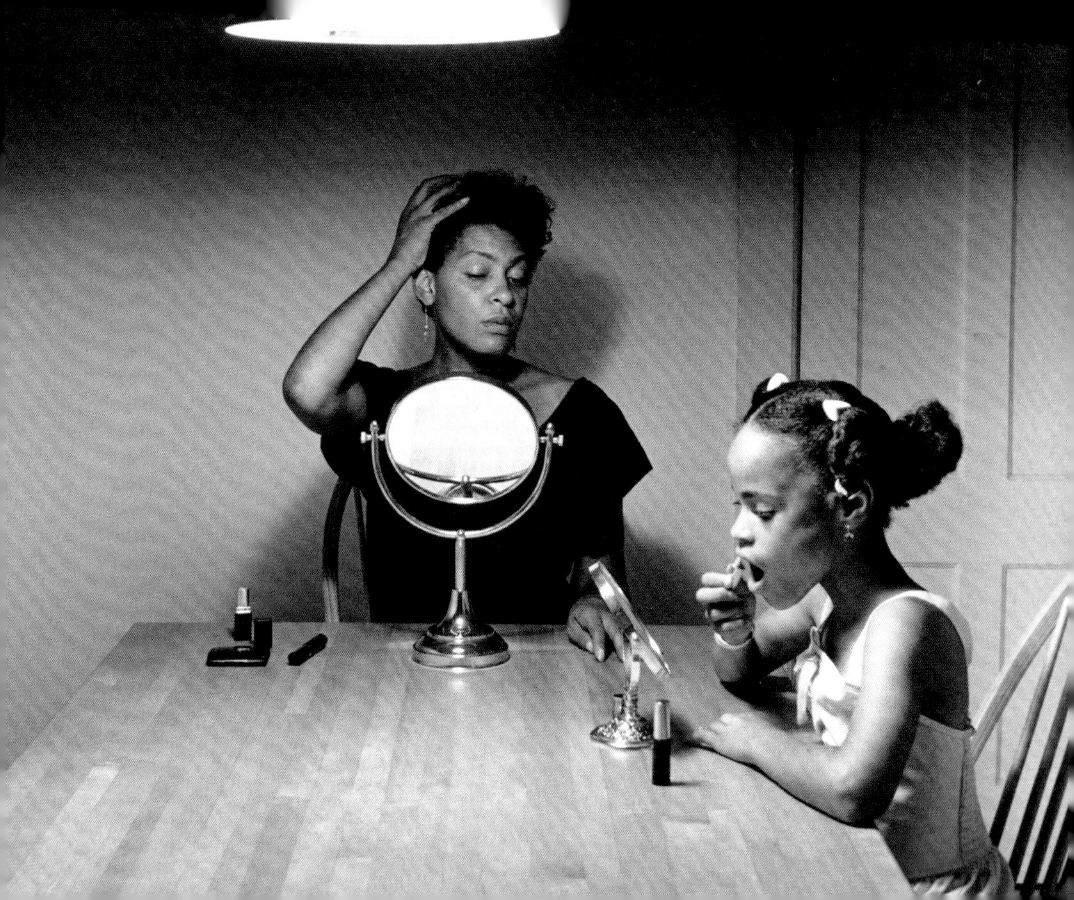

Art has saved my life on a regular basis.

Carrie Mae Weems

A dream you dream alone may be a dream, but a dream two people dream together is a reality.

Yoko Ono

Don't be
intimidated
about anything.

Carmen Herrera

We are all the living ends of very, very long threads.

Jeffrey Gibson

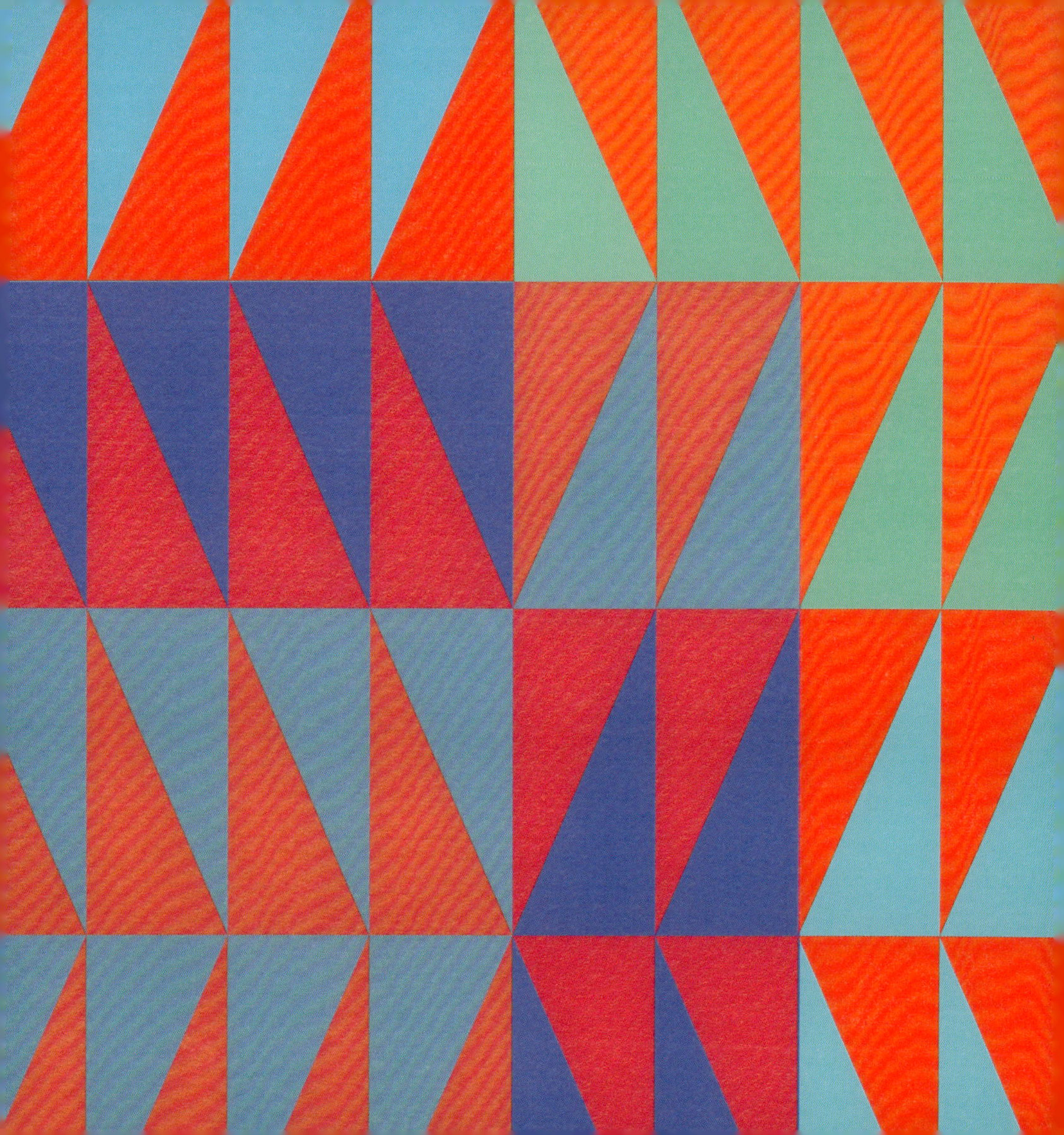

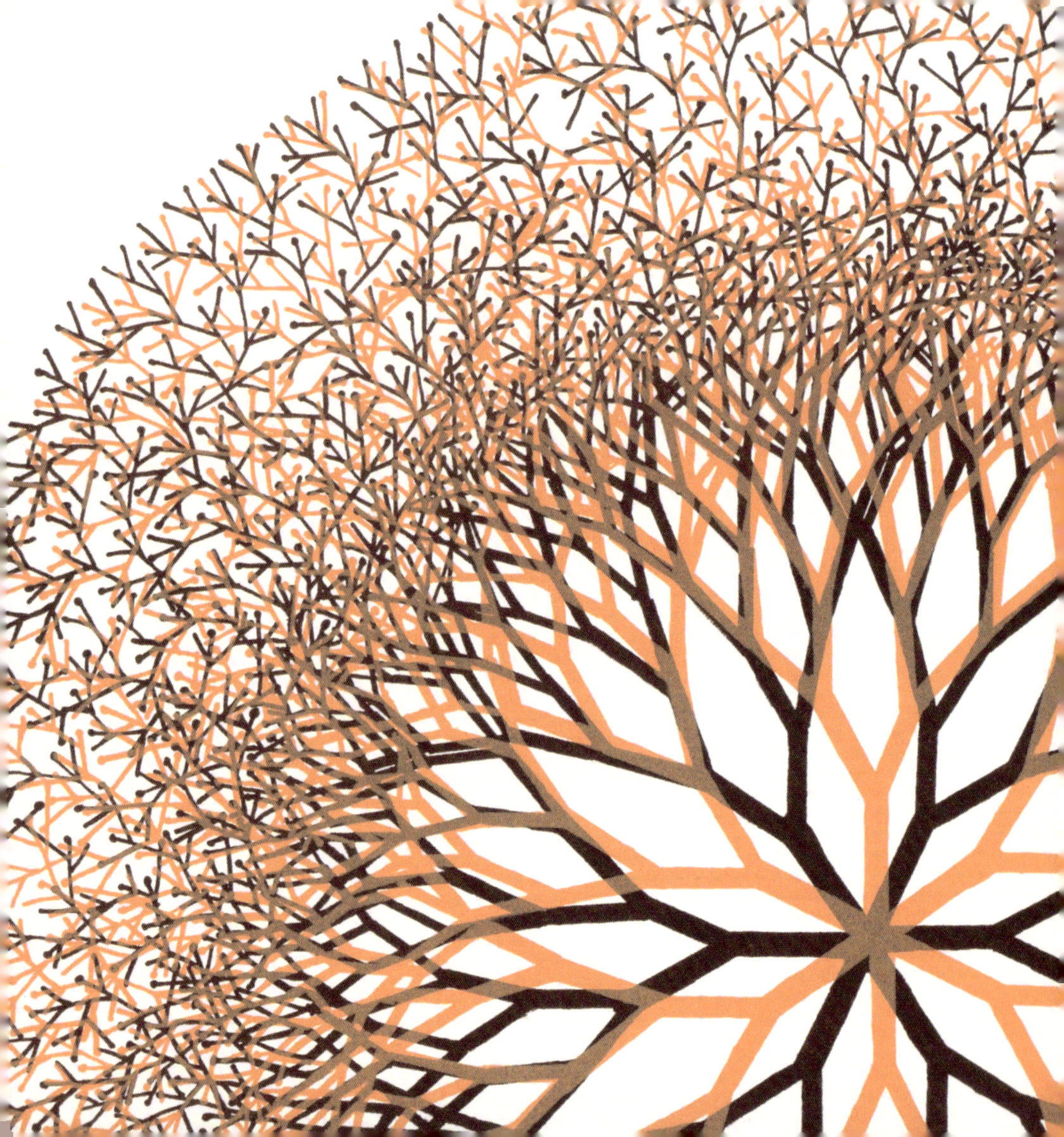

Above everything be curious, learn all you can, and take a lifetime doing it.

Ruth Asawa

Illustrations

All works are in the collection of The Museum of Modern Art, New York. Many images throughout the book are details.

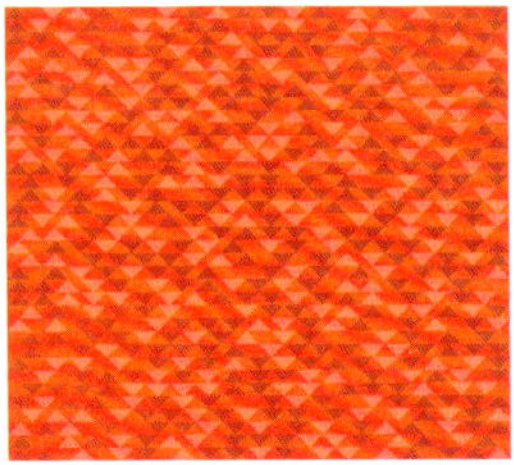

Anni Albers (American, born Germany. 1899–1994)
TR I. 1969, published 1970
Lithograph, comp.: 14 × 16 in. (35.6 × 40.6 cm); sheet: 19¹³⁄₁₆ × 21⅞ in. (50.3 × 55.6 cm)
Publisher and printer: Gemini G.E.L., Los Angeles
Edition: 44
Gift of Gemini G.E.L.

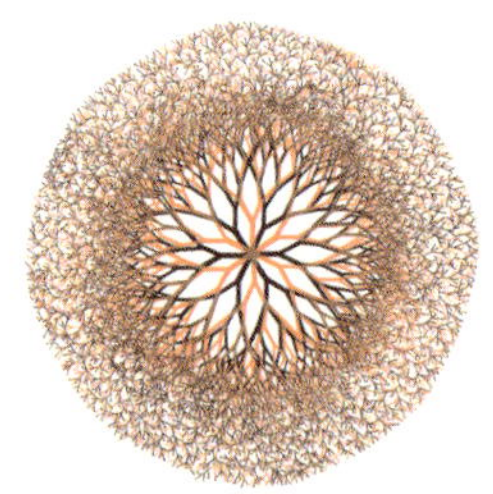

Ruth Asawa (American, 1926–2013)
Desert Flower (TAM.1460-II). 1965
Lithograph, comp. (irreg.):
17⁷⁄₁₆ × 17½ in. (44.3 × 44.5 cm); sheet: 18⁹⁄₁₆ × 18⁹⁄₁₆ in. (47.1 × 47.1 cm)
Publisher and printer: Tamarind Lithography Workshop, Inc., Los Angeles
Edition: proof outside the edition of 10
Gift of Kleiner, Bell & Co.

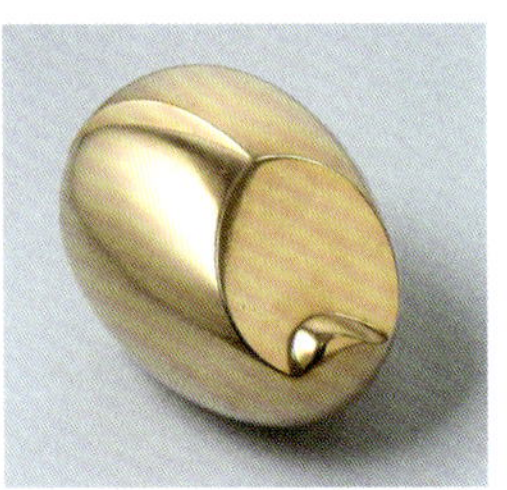

Constantin Brancusi (French, born Romania. 1876–1957)
The Newborn. Version I, 1920
Bronze, 5¾ × 8¼ × 5¾ in. (14.6 × 21 × 14.6 cm)
Acquired through the Lillie P. Bliss Bequest (by exchange)

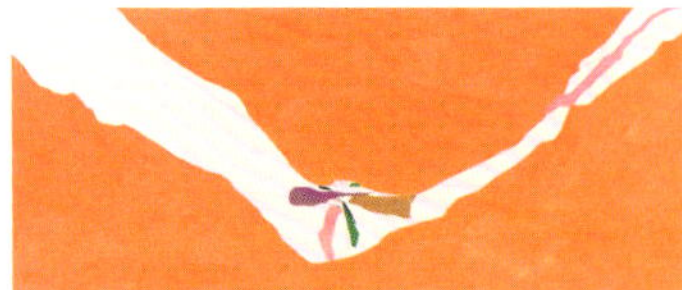

Helen Frankenthaler (American, 1928–2011)
Chairman of the Board. 1971
Acrylic and felt-tip pen on canvas, 6 ft. 10¹⁄₁₆ in. × 16 ft. 2⁵⁄₁₆ in. (208.4 × 493.6 cm)
Nina and Gordon Bunshaft Bequest

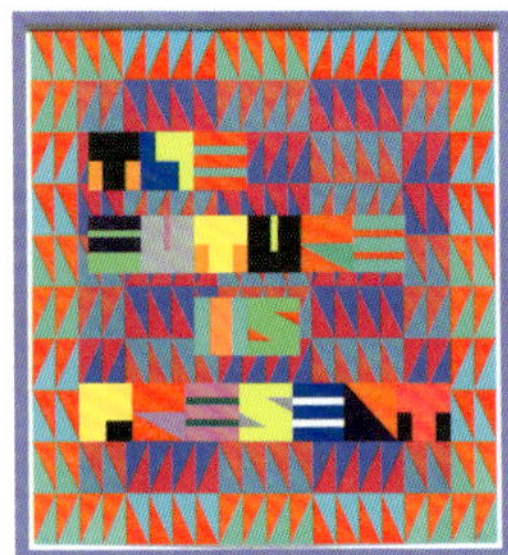

Jeffrey Gibson (American, member of the Mississippi Band of Choctaw Indians and Cherokee, born 1972)
THE FUTURE IS PRESENT. 2019

Screenprint on inkjet print with
cut-and-pasted printed paper in
artist's frame, frame: 40 ½ ×
36 ⅝ in. (102.9 × 93 cm); sheet:
38 × 34 in. (96.5 × 86.4 cm)
Publisher: Sikkema Jenkins & Co.,
New York
Printer: Lower East Side
Printshop, New York
Edition: 30
Fund for the Twenty-First Century

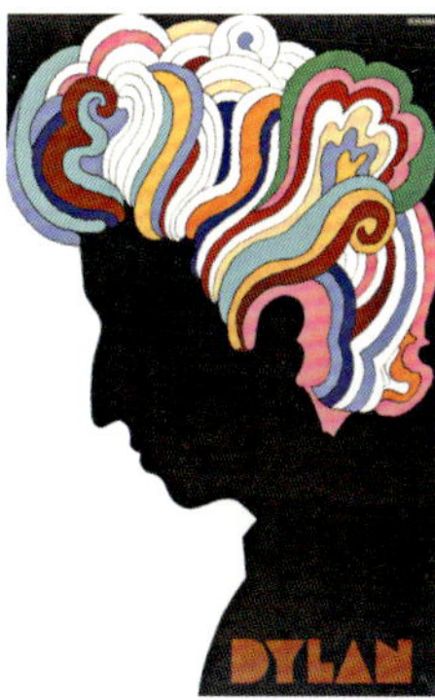

Milton Glaser (American,
1929–2020)
Dylan. 1966
Offset lithograph, 33 × 22 in.
(83.8 × 55.9 cm)
Gift of the designer

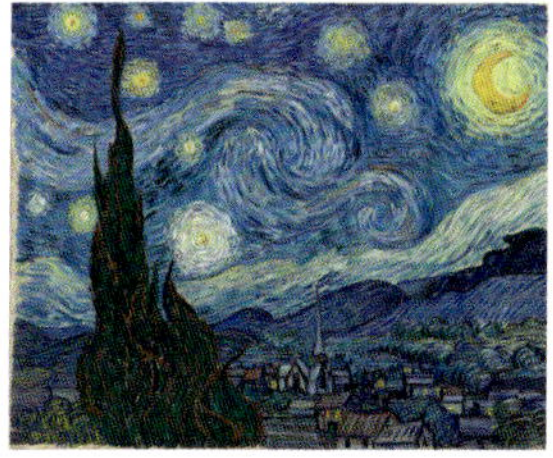

Vincent van Gogh (Dutch,
1853–1890)
The Starry Night. 1889
Oil on canvas, 29 × 36 ¼ in.
(73.7 × 92.1 cm)
Acquired through the Lillie P. Bliss
Bequest (by exchange)

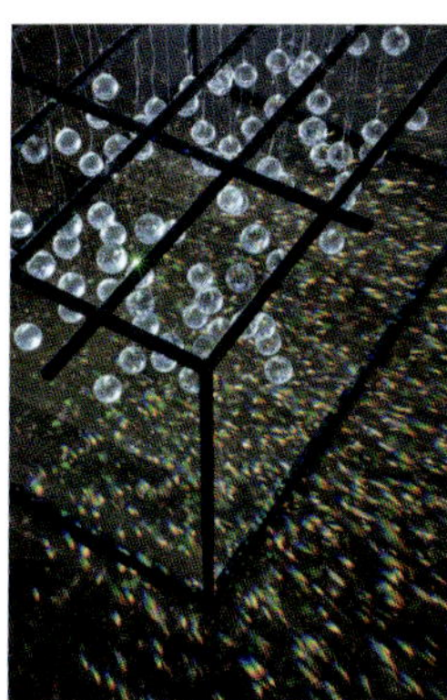

Joan Jonas (American, born 1936)
Reanimation. 2010/2012/2013
Multimedia installation with four
videos (color, sound and silent)

projected on custom screens;
prefabricated house structure;
two benches made by Ed Gavagan;
crystal sculpture; two video sculptures with wood, trestles, and
video (*Under the Glacier* [color,
sound; 18:33 min.] and *Fish* [color,
silent; 8:51 min.]); fifteen ink
drawings on paper; three oil stick
drawings on paper; and two china
marker wall drawings. Soundtrack
and voice: Joan Jonas. Sámi
yoik singing: Ánde Somby. Piano
and additional sound effects:
Jason Moran. Varying durations.
Dimensions variable.
Acquired in part through The
Modern Women's Fund

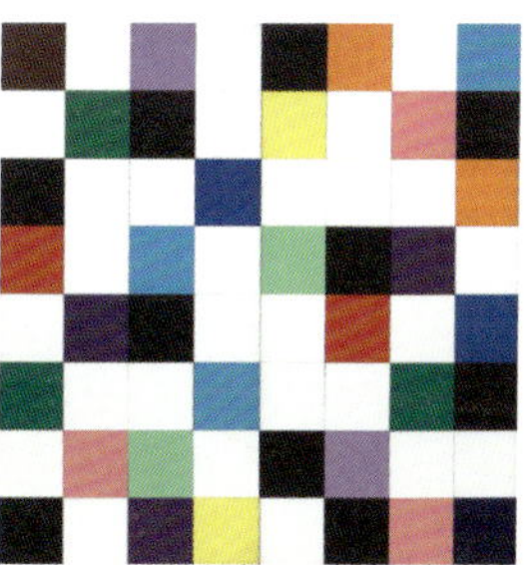

Ellsworth Kelly (American,
1923–2015)
Colors for a Large Wall. 1951
Oil on canvas, sixty-four panels,
7 ft. 10 ¼ in. × 7 ft. 6 ½ in.
(239.4 × 229.9 cm)
Gift of the artist

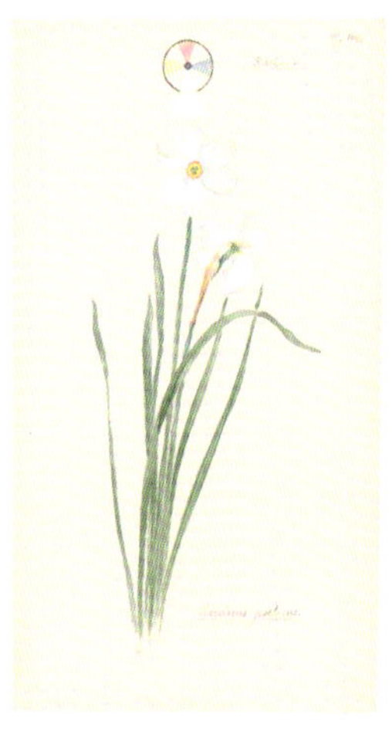

Hilma af Klint (Swedish, 1862–1944)
Narcissus poeticus (Poet's Narcissus), sheet 34 from *Nature Studies*. 1920
Watercolor, pencil, ink, gouache, and metallic paint on paper, sheet (irreg.): 19½ × 10⅝ in. (49.5 × 27 cm)
Committee on Drawings and Prints Fund and gift of Jack Shear

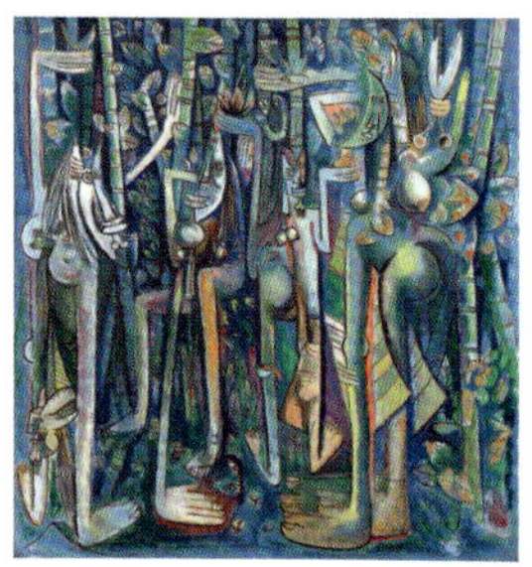

Wifredo Lam (Cuban, 1902–1982)
La jungla (The Jungle). 1942–43
Oil and charcoal on paper mounted on canvas, 7 ft. 10 ¼ in. × 7 ft. 6 ½ in. (239.4 × 229.9 cm)
Inter-American Fund

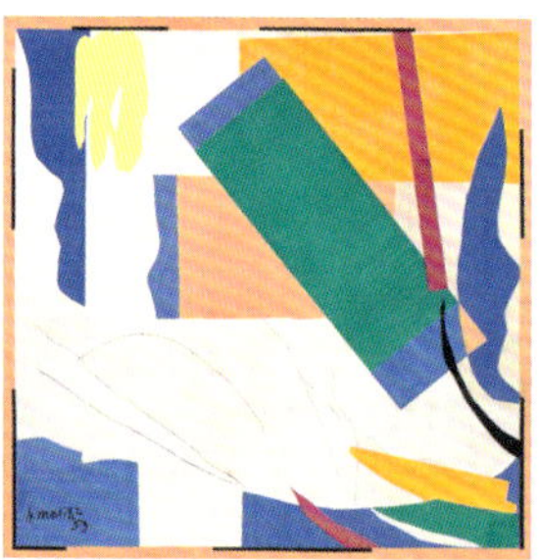

Henri Matisse (French, 1869–1954)
Memory of Oceania. 1952–53
Gouache on paper, cut and pasted, and charcoal on paper mounted on canvas, 9 ft. 4 in. × 9 ft. 4 ⅞ in. (284.5 × 286.7 cm)
Mrs. Simon Guggenheim Fund

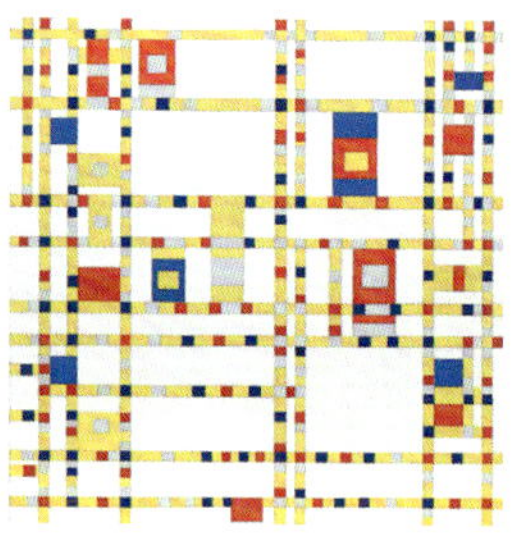

Piet Mondrian (Dutch, 1872–1944)
Broadway Boogie Woogie. 1942–43
Oil on canvas, 50 × 50 in. (127 × 127 cm)
Given anonymously

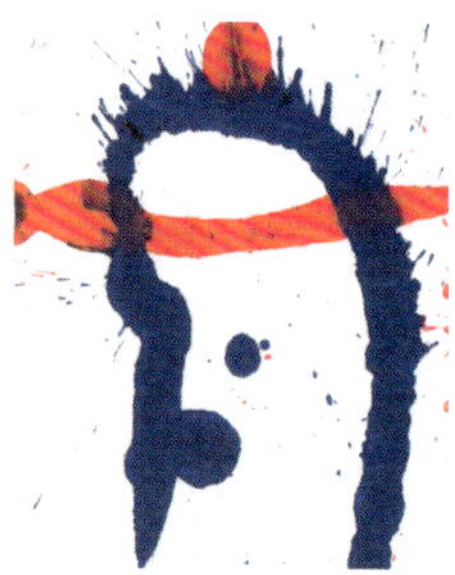

Robert Motherwell (American, 1915–1991)
Untitled from Lyric Suite. 1965
Colored ink on paper, 11 ⅛ × 9 in. (28.3 × 22.9 cm)
Gift of the artist in memory of Frank O'Hara

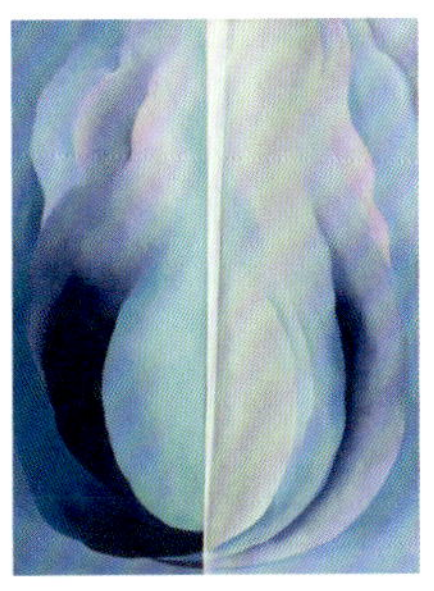

Georgia O'Keeffe (American, 1887–1986)
Abstraction Blue. 1927
Oil on canvas, 40 ¼ × 30 in.
(102.2 × 76.2 cm)
Acquired through the Helen
Acheson Bequest

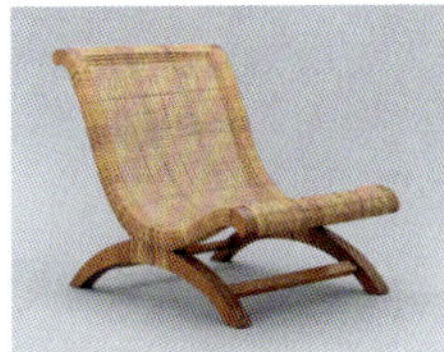

Clara Porset (Mexican, born Cuba.
1895–1981)
Butaque. c. 1957
Laminated wood and woven
wicker, 28 ¾ × 25 ¹³⁄₁₆ × 33 ⁷⁄₁₆ in.
(73 × 65.6 × 84.9 cm)
Gift of The Modern Women's Fund

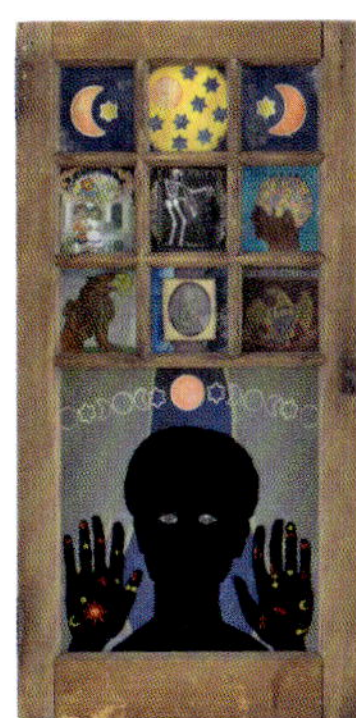

Betye Saar (American, born 1926)
Black Girl's Window. 1969
Wooden window frame with
paint, cut-and-pasted printed and
painted papers, daguerreotype,
lenticular print, and plastic
figurine, 35 ¾ × 18 × 1 ½ in.
(90.8 × 45.7 × 3.8 cm)
Gift of Candace King Weir through
The Modern Women's Fund
and Committee on Painting and
Sculpture Funds

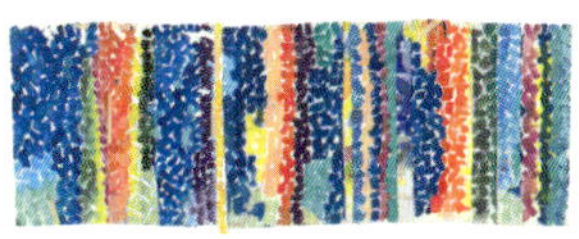

Alma Woodsey Thomas
(American, 1891–1978)
Untitled. c. 1968
Acrylic and pressure-sensitive
tape on cut-and-stapled paper,
19 ⅛ × 51 ½ in. (48.6 × 130.8 cm)
Gift of Donald B. Marron

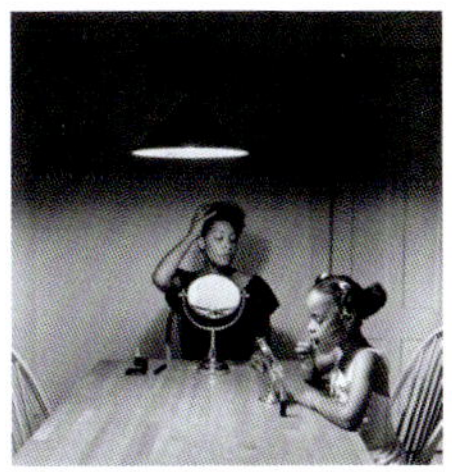

Carrie Mae Weems (American,
born 1953)
*Untitled (woman and daughter
with makeup)*. 1990
Gelatin silver print, printed 2010,
10 × 10 in. (25.4 × 25.4 cm)
Gift of Light Work, Carrie Mae
Weems, and Robert B. Menschel

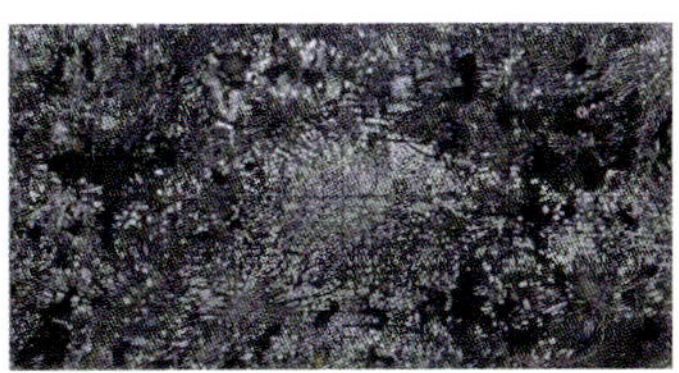

Jack Whitten (American, 1939–2018)
Atopolis: For Édouard Glissant. 2014
Acrylic on canvas, eight panels,
overall: 10 ft. 4 ½ in. × 20 ft. 8 ½ in.
(316.2 × 631.2 cm)
Acquired through the generosity of
Sid R. Bass, Lonti Ebers, Agnes Gund,
Henry and Marie-Josée Kravis,
Jerry Speyer and Katherine Farley,
and Daniel and Brett Sundheim

Sources

Anni Albers, oral history interview, July 5, 1968, Archives of American Art, Smithsonian Institution.

Ruth Asawa to Alicia Schultz, April 25, 1972, Ruth Asawa Papers, series 7, box 127, folder 2, statements 1972–74, Stanford Special Collections, Stanford University Libraries.

Louise Bourgeois, in Louise Bourgeois with Lawrence Rinder, *Louise Bourgeois: Drawings and Observations* (University Art Museum and Pacific Film Archive, University of California, Berkeley; Bulfinch, 1995), 48. © 2026 The Easton Foundation/Artists Rights Society (ARS), New York

Constantin Brancusi, "Selected Aphorisms," in *Constantin Brancusi: The Essence of Things*, ed. Carmen Gimenez and Matthew Gale (Tate, 2004), 133.

John Cage, interview by Richard Kostelanetz, "Esthetics," in *Conversing with Cage* (Limelight Editions, 1994), 207. © John Cage Trust

Marcel Duchamp, "The Creative Act," *ARTnews* 56, no. 4 (Summer 1957): 29.

© Association Marcel Duchamp/ADAGP, Paris/Artists Rights Society (ARS), New York 2026

Charles and Ray Eames, in Eames Demetrios, "Take Your Pleasure Seriously," in *An Eames Primer* (Rizzoli, 2013), 122. © 2026 Eames Office, LLC. All rights reserved

Helen Frankenthaler, oral history interview, 1968, Archives of American Art, Smithsonian Institution.

LaToya Ruby Frazier, "On Working with Dignity," interview by Daniel Sharp, *Creative Independent*, September 11, 2020, thecreativeindependent.com/people/visual-artist-latoya-ruby-fraizer-on-working-with-dignity/.

Jeffrey Gibson, interview by Anthony Hudson, *BOMB Magazine*, no. 168 (Summer 2024): 32.

Milton Glaser, in Anne McColl, "A Call to Action with Milton Glaser," *Communication Arts*, n.d., commarts.com/columns/a-call-to-action-with-milton-glaser.

Vincent van Gogh to Theo van Gogh, April 30, 1874, inv. no. b16 V/1962, Van Gogh Museum, Amsterdam. Trans. at vangoghletters.org/vg/letters/let022/letter.html.

Carmen Herrera, in Andrew Russeth, "'Don't Be Intimidated About Anything': Carmen Herrera at 100," *ARTnews* (online), June 5, 2015.

Eva Hesse, interview by Cindy Nemser, *Artforum* 8, no. 9 (May 1970): 60.

Joan Jonas, "Journeys," in *In the Shadow a Shadow: The Work of Joan Jonas*, ed. Joan Simon (Gregory R. Miller, 2015), 481.

Ellsworth Kelly, "Notes from 1969," in *Ellsworth Kelly: Paintings and Sculptures 1963–1979* (Stedelijk Museum, 1979), 34.

Hilma af Klint, *Studier over själslivet*, unpublished manuscript, 1917–18, 1941–42, 1151, Hilma af Klint Foundation, Stockholm. Trans. Henrik Essunger and Fredrika Klay, Eriksen Translations.

Wifredo Lam, in Max-Pol Fouchet, "Depths of the Jungle," chap. 11 in *Wifredo Lam* (Ediciones Polígrafa, 1976), 189.

An-My Lê, interview by Hilton Als, in *Small Wars* (Aperture, 2005), 121.

Christian Marclay, in David Fear, "The Clock's Christian Marclay," *TimeOut* (online), July 10, 2012.

Henri Matisse, interview by André Verdet (1952), chap. 42 in *Matisse on Art*, ed. Jack D. Flam (Dutton, 1978), 143.

Piet Mondrian, in Carl Holty, "Mondrian in New York: A Memoir," *Arts* 31, no. 10 (September 1957): 21.

Robert Motherwell to Frank O'Hara, August 18, 1965, in *Robert Motherwell* (The Museum of Modern Art, 1965), 67.

Georgia O'Keeffe, The Museum of Modern Art, "Paintings of Georgia O'Keeffe Shown in Retrospective at Museum of Modern Art," press release, 1946, MoMA Press Release Archives, The Museum of Modern Art Archives, New York.

Yoko Ono, *Grapefruit* (Simon and Schuster, 1970), n.p.

Neri Oxman, in Nick Compton, "Under the Skin of MIT's Magical Mask Maker Neri Oxman," *Wired* (online), September 9, 2016.

Nam June Paik, in Thérèse Beyler, entry for Paik's *A Tribute to John Cage* (1973), n.d., trans. Anna Knight, New Media Collection @ Centre Pompidou, https://www.newmedia-art.org/cgi-bin/show-oeu.php?IDO=150000000034528&LG=GBR&ALP=P.

Pope.L, *Hole Theory: Parts 4 and 5* (pub. by author, 2002), n.p. Courtesy the Estate of Pope.L and Mitchell-Innes & Nash, New York. © The Estate of Pope.L

Liubov Popova, "Documents," in John E. Bowlt and Matthew Drutt, *Amazons of the Avant-Garde: Alexandra Exter, Natalia Goncharova, Liubov Popova, Olga Rozanova, Varvara Stepanova, and Nadezhda Udaltsova* (Guggenheim Museum, 2000), 321.

Clara Porset, "¿Qué es diseño?," *Arquitectura México*, no. 28 (1949): 170. Trans. Amanda Forment. Courtesy Archivo Clara Porset, Centro de Investigaciones de Diseño Industrial (CIDI), Facultad de Arquitectura (FA), Universidad Nacional Autónoma de México (UNAM)

Ed Ruscha, in Fred Fehlau, "Ed Ruscha," *Flash Art*, no. 138 (January–February 1988): 70.

Betye Saar, "How I Became an Artist," as told to Janelle Zara, *Art Basel*, n.d., artbasel.com/stories/betye-saar-interview-ica-miami.

Malick Sidibé, "Malick Sidibé Photographs: One Nation Under a Groove," interview by Jon Henley, *Guardian* (online), February 26, 2010.

Ettore Sottsass, in "A Conversation About the Good, the Bad, and the Ugly," moderated by Chee Pearlman, *Wired* (online), January 1, 2001. © Erede Ettore Sottsass/Artists Rights Society, New York, 2026

Alma Woodsey Thomas, "The Late Spring Time of Alma Thomas," interview by Eleanor Munro, *Washington Post* (online), April 14, 1979.

Guillermo del Toro, "Death Is the Curator," interview by Lauren Wilford, *Bright Wall/Dark Room* (online), no. 44 (February 2017).

Carrie Mae Weems, "Artist Carrie Mae Weems on 30 Years of Genius," interview by #Team EBONY, *Ebony* (online), February 5, 2014.

Jack Whitten, "Space as Object," in *Jack Whitten: Notes from the Woodshed*, ed. Katy Siegel (Hauser and Wirth, 2018), 291.

Select URLs have been provided for clarity.

Image Credits

In reproducing the images contained in this publication, the Museum obtained the permission of the rights holders whenever possible. If, notwithstanding good-faith efforts, the Museum could not locate the rights holders, it requests that any contact information concerning such rights holders be forwarded so that they may be contacted for future editions.

MoMA publications are made possible by the Helen and Sam Zell Publications Fund.

Leadership support for this publication is provided by the Kate W. Cassidy Foundation.

Produced by the Department of Publications, The Museum of Modern Art, New York

Michelle Kuo, Chief Curator at Large and Publisher
Curtis R. Scott, Associate Publisher
Hannah Kim, Business and Marketing Director
Joseph Mohan, Production Director
Anna Barnet, Managing Editor

Edited by Sophie Golub
Designed by Amanda Washburn, with Juliana Maurer
Production by Matthew Pimm
Research by Julia Brukx
Proofread by Jeffrey Castle
Printed and bound by Ofset Yapımevi, Istanbul

This book is typeset in MoMA Sans. The paper is 170 gsm Magno Volume.

Published by The Museum of Modern Art
11 West 53 Street
New York, NY 10019
moma.org

Library of Congress Control Number: 2026935661
ISBN: 978-1-63345-189-6

Distributed in the United States and Canada by
ARTBOOK | D.A.P.
75 Broad Street, Suite 630
New York, NY 10004
artbook.com

Distributed outside the United States and Canada by
Thames & Hudson
6-24 Britannia Street
London WC1X 9JD
thamesandhudson.com

Front endpaper: Alma Woodsey Thomas. Untitled. c. 1968. Front flyleaf: Anni Albers. *TR I*. 1969, published 1970. Back flyleaf: Helen Frankenthaler. *Chairman of the Board*. 1971. Back endpaper: Jack Whitten. *Atopolis: For Édouard Glissant*. 2014

Printed in Turkey

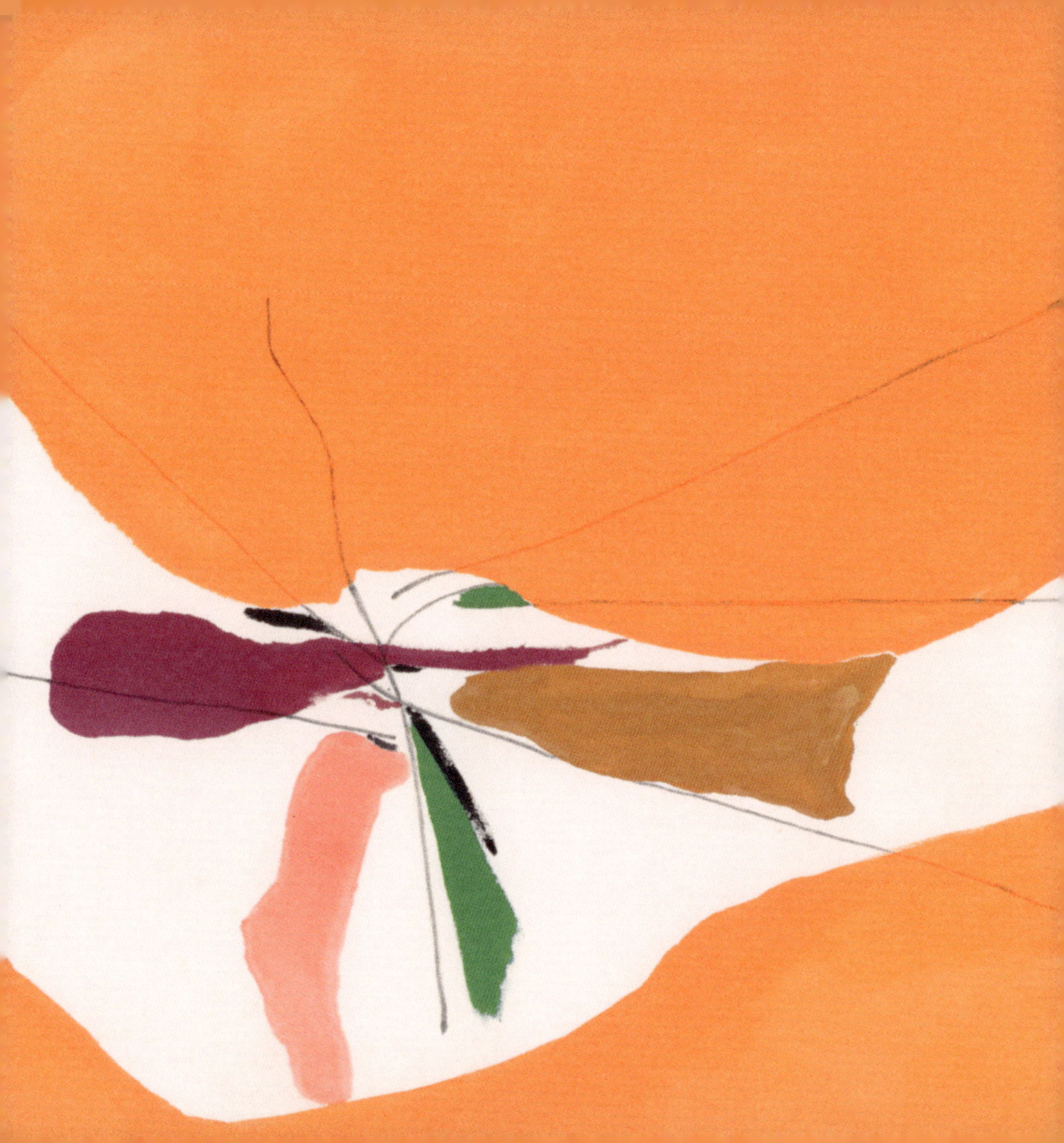

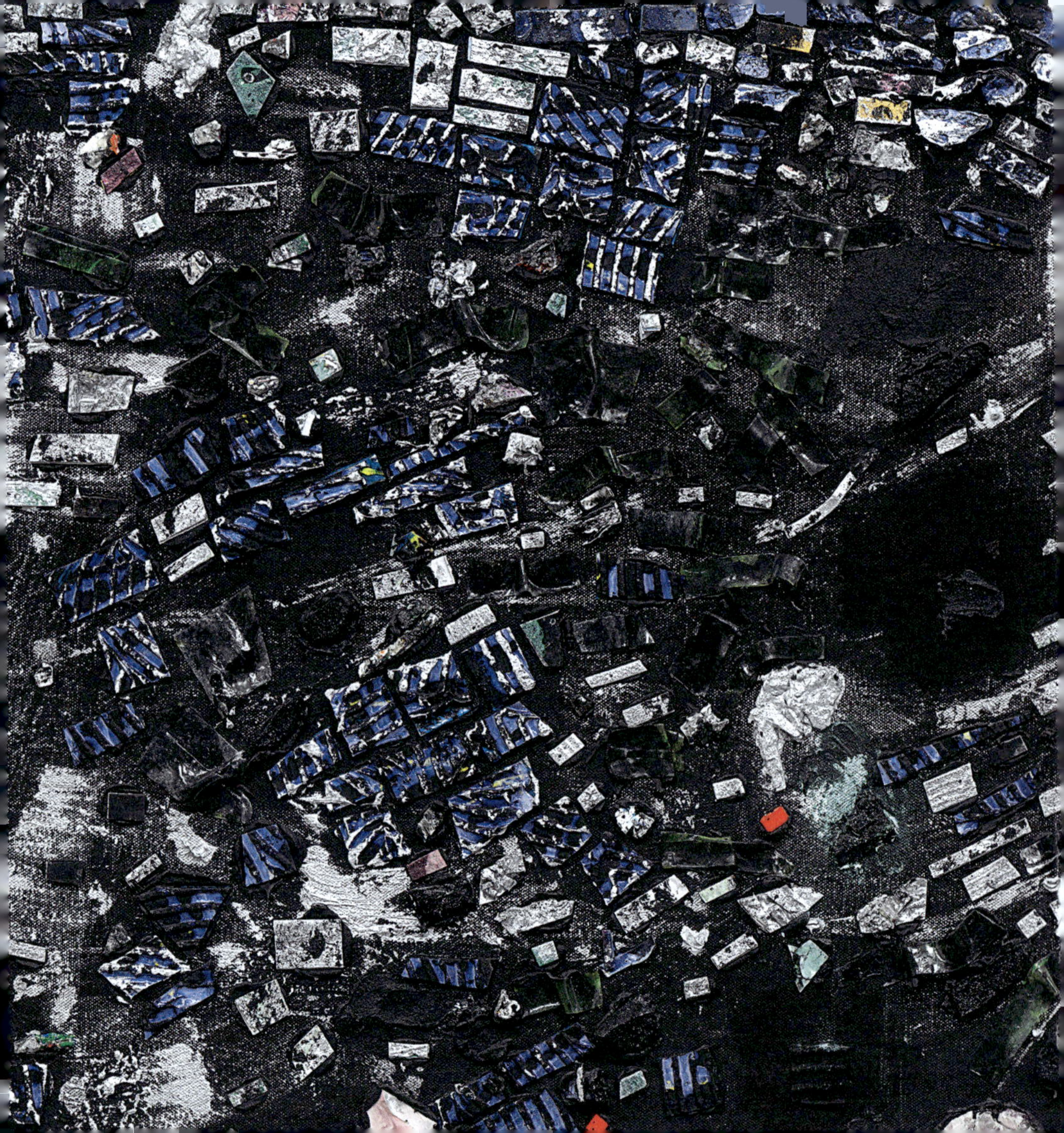